D1377356

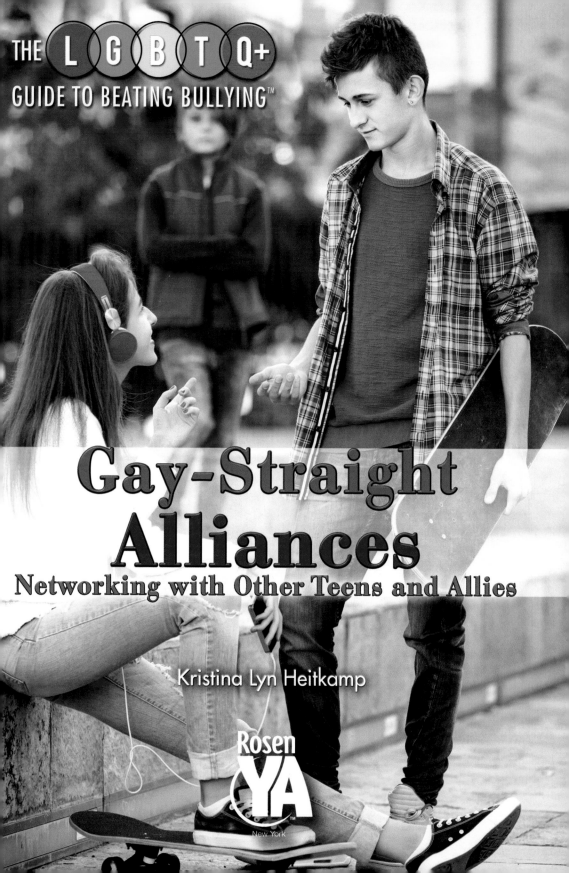

THE **L G B T Q**+
GUIDE TO BEATING BULLYING™

Gay-Straight
Alliances
Networking with Other Teens and Allies

Kristina Lyn Heitkamp

Rosen
YA
New York

To my brother Charles Wesley Larsen

Published in 2018 by The Rosen Publishing Group, Inc.
29 East 21st Street, New York, NY 10010

Copyright © 2018 by The Rosen Publishing Group, Inc.

First Edition

Library of Congress Cataloging-in-Publication Data

Names: Heitkamp, Kristina Lyn, author.
Title: Gay-straight alliances : networking with other teens and allies / Kristina Lyn Heitkamp.
Description: New York : Rosen Publishing, 2018 | Series: The LGBTQ+ guide to beating bullying | Includes bibliographical references and index. | Audience: Grades 7–12.
Identifiers: LCCN 2016056447 | ISBN 9781508174271 (library bound book) | ISBN 9781508174264 (pbk. book) | ISBN 9781508174615 (6 pack)
Subjects: LCSH: Gay high school students—Societies, etc.—Handbooks, manuals, etc. | Sexual minority students—Societies, etc.—Handbooks, manuals, etc. | High school environment—Handbooks, manuals, etc. | School management and organization—Handbooks, manuals, etc. | Gay rights—Handbooks, manuals, etc.
Classification: LCC LC2574.5 .H45 2018 | DDC 373.1826/64—dc23
LC record available at https://lccn.loc.gov/2016056447

Manufactured in the United States of America

CONTENTS

INTRODUCTION

In 1989, a ninth grader at Concord Academy in Concord, Massachusetts, decided she'd had enough. Her name was Meredith, and she was sick and tired of all the bullying at her school. One winter morning she decided to do something about it. She went to her history teacher, Kevin Jennings, with a proposal—she wanted to start a club to fight homophobia at the school. Jennings had recently come out as a gay man to the school administration and students, which was a rare thing in those days.

Julia Davidson, copresident of the gay-straight alliance at a Portland, Maine, high school speaks at a meeting of the club. Maine has more than seventy GSAs in high schools in several different counties.

Jennings was delighted but a little surprised by Meredith's request. As far as he knew, she did not identify as LGBTQ+—an acronym for those who identify as gay, lesbian, bisexual, transgender, or any other minority sexual or gender identity. He knew Meredith had a boyfriend at the school and had always assumed Meredith was straight. He told Meredith that he'd be happy to help, but asked why she wanted to start a club. She said her mom was a lesbian, and she was tired of hearing hurtful remarks about her family. Jennings was intrigued with her idea as he hadn't thought about that angle. Meredith asked if he would sign on as the faculty adviser for the group. He agreed, and it was decided since she was straight, and he was gay, they would call the club gay-straight alliances.

Little did Meredith and Jennings know that their action would start a movement that has changed the lives of many LGBTQ+ youth around the world. Gay-straight alliance (GSA) clubs have popped up all over the United States in thousands of schools and communities, offering a safe and supportive environment for LGBTQ+ youth as well as their family and friends.

Kevin Jennings went on to found the Gay, Lesbian & Straight Education Network (GLSEN), a national education organization. GLSEN is focused on putting an end to bullying and harassment, and ensuring safe schools for all students, regardless of their sexual orientation or gender identity and expression. The organization also offers support to gay-straight alliances through guidebooks, resources, and a GSA national registration.

Since their humble beginnings, GSAs have proved their ability to create safe and inclusive climates. A 2016 Vanderbilt University study surveyed nearly sixty-three thousand US high school students and found that 52 percent of LGBTQ+ students in a school with a GSA were less likely to hear homophobic remarks. In addition, 36 percent were less likely to be fearful for their personal safety. But that's not all. The presence of a GSA was also linked to lower levels of victimization for all students, whether they identified as LGBTQ+ or straight and regardless of whether they participated in the club. A GSA sends a message to students and staff that their school is a safe place where bullying and harassment will not be tolerated.

Whether gay, lesbian, bisexual, transgender, straight, cisgender, or any other sexual orientation or gender identity, GSAs are a place where students can come to ask questions, talk about daily challenges, and build strength to advocate for human rights in their community and beyond.

CHAPTER ONE

THE MANY FACES OF LGBTQ+

The LGBTQ+ community represents a diverse population of people, from different backgrounds, ages and ethnicities. But what exactly do the letters mean? LGBTQ+ is an acronym for lesbian, gay, bisexual, transgender, queer or questioning, and the plus sign indicates other identities in the community. These terms refer to a person's sexual orientation or gender identity. The following descriptions offer a basic understanding that can be built upon and further explored. But just as sexual or gender identity can shift over time, the definitions are also open to change.

Lesbian, Gay, Bisexual

During the sixth century, a Greek poet named Sappho lived on the island of Lesbos. She wrote lyrical poems about life and love, especially romantic love between women. Sappho's life and creative works later became a symbol of female homosexuality. The term "lesbian" is derived from Sappho of Lesbos. A lesbian is an individual who identifies as a woman and who is emotionally, physically, and/or sexually attracted to other women.

The word "gay" has a few different meanings. The term defines a person as lighthearted and carefree, or it can refer to someone's sexual orientation. Gay describes an individual who identifies as

Lesbian couples, like the one shown here, earned the right to marry when the United States Supreme Court ruled on June 26, 2015, that same-sex marriage is legal in the United States.

a man, and who is emotionally, physically, and/or sexually attracted to other men. It is also used as an umbrella word to include all LGBTQ+ people. Bisexual, or sometimes just bi, is someone who is emotionally, physically, and/or sexually attracted to both males and females. An individual who is interested in same-sex relationships is described as bicurious. People can closely identify with a specific sexual orientation, or they may fall somewhere on the spectrum.

T Stands for Transgender

Each human has a biological sex—whether they are male, female, or intersex. Intersex is used to describe an individual who has genetic, hormonal, and physical features associated with both males and females. But a person's gender identity is completely unrelated to their biological anatomy or even their sexual orien-

tation. What it means to be transgender is often misunderstood. "Transgender" is a comprehensive term used to describe people whose gender identity is inconsistent with the gender they were assigned at birth. A transgender man is a person who identifies as a man but was assigned female at birth, such as the celebrity activist Chaz Bono. A transgender woman is an individual who identifies as a woman but was assigned male at birth, such as the Emmy-nominated TV star Laverne Cox. Cisgender is someone whose gender identity is consistent with the gender they were assigned at birth.

LGBTQ+ activist Chaz Bono attends the 2014 Gay & Lesbian Mardi Gras VIP Party in Sydney, Australia. Bono brought awareness to LGBTQ+ issues when he came out as transgender.

"Genderqueer" is another umbrella term that refers to gender identities that fall outside the gender binary. The gender binary is the idea that there are only two genders that all people must fall into, either male or female. But the word genderqueer recognizes that gender identity is a fluid concept and some people may combine both male and female aspects. Don't assume someone's gender identity based on what you think or even what you see, such as how they are dressed or how they act. The best advice is to ask how they identify, including what pronouns they prefer.

The Q+ in LGBTQ+

Humans are complex beings with a fantastic ability to self-evaluate and understand their place in the world. And because humans are not robots, we do not all prescribe to the exact same identity. Q stands for queer or questioning, and the plus sign represents other identities in the community.

Queer is a comprehensive term that relates to the entire LGBTQ+ community. Q also stands for questioning. Questioning refers to someone who is exploring their gender and sexual identities or gender expression. The plus sign is used in order to include all identities and to ensure that everyone feels welcome and recognized and that nobody is left out. Whether you identify as gender variant, asexual, or bigender, there's a spot for you in the LGBTQ+ community.

Gender variant, such as agender, bigender, or pangender, describes an individual who does not correspond to binary

Members of Millwood High School's gay-straight alliance club show their pride as they participate in the twenty-fifth annual Halifax Pride Parade in Halifax, Nova Scotia.

gender-based expectations of society. Agender refers to a person who does not identify with any gender. Also sometimes called genderless, genderfree, or non-gendered, agender individuals are those who do not conform to traditional gender norms. Bigender describes someone who moves between female and male gender identity, expressions, and behavior. They also will identify as two genders simultaneously. Those who relate to all genders are called pangender.

UNDERSTANDING IDENTITY

With all the different terms available to define and better understand your identity, it can sometimes get confusing. Occasionally sex and gender identity are lumped together and thought to be one and the same. That is not the case, however. A person's biological sex is generally assigned at birth by their anatomic appearance or physiological parameters. An individual's gender is a conclusion based on personal gender identity, expression, or behavior. Sexual and gender identity are also sometimes thought to be indistinguishable from each other. This, too, is not correct. Sexual identity develops beyond childhood.

Sexual orientation refers to being romantically or sexually attracted to a specific gender, but is completely separate from gender identity. Gender identity is an individual's intuitive sense of gender. It can be how a person understands themselves in terms of gender, how they relate to others, or even how they choose to show themselves to the world. It is a personal conception of oneself as male or female and sometimes both or neither.

Gender identity is also the outward expression of gender, such as behavior and appearance. For example, if a person identifies as male and he is most comfortable with referring to his personal gender in masculine terms, then his gender identity is male. An individual's experience of gender identity or sexual orientation may shift over time, as they better understand themselves. A person may not firmly know their sexual orientation or gender identity, and that's OK. These things take time to discover—and even then, they sometimes change.

Other possible identities found in the LGBTQ+ community are asexual and pansexual. Asexual is used to describe an individual who lacks sexual attraction to anyone or who has very little to no interest in sexual activities. Pansexual refers to a person who is emotionally, romantically, physically, and sexually attracted to all members of gender identities or expressions, or any sex. Some people who identify as pansexual may say that they are gender-blind, believing that gender and sex are irrelevant when it comes to attraction and love. The American singer, songwriter, and actor Miley Cyrus is pansexual.

What Is an Ally?

However a person identifies, they can be an ally to the LGBTQ+ community. Allies are individuals or groups, like a gay-straight alliance club (GSA). An ally is a friend and an advocate. A teen or adult can be an ally. Allyship is a partnership that allows members to learn from one another while in pursuit of a common goal. But most of all, allies believe in the human rights of the LGBTQ+ community. Allies take action to support and respect the many faces of LGBTQ+. They set an example for their school and community. Working together, allies strive to make schools more inclusive and safe from harassment and bullying.

Several celebrities have stood tall and proud as allies to the LGBTQ+ community, including star of *The Hunger Games* Josh Hutcherson, Grammy award winner Lady Gaga, and Olympian Chris Mosier. Allies, gay or straight, can be effective and powerful voices in the LGBTQ+ movement.

CHAPTER TWO

SAFE SPACE

Schools are responsible for maintaining a safe learning environment for all students. However, many LGBTQ+ youth feel that school is a dangerous and unwelcoming place. LGBTQ+ students are bullied and harassed, making it a challenge to stay in school. GSAs are there to help. But what exactly is a GSA?

A Port in the Storm

Some dub it Rainbow or Pride Club, while others call it Gender Sexuality Alliance. Known by many names, a gay-straight alliance (GSA) is a student-organized and student-run club in a public or private school. GSAs are also created in communities, but most clubs are found in middle schools, high schools, and college campuses. The main goal of a GSA is to provide a safe space for LGBTQ+ students and their allies. The alliance is just like any other school club, with a faculty adviser, regular meetings, and activities.

GSAs have an open door policy. All students are welcome, however they identify. Students with LGBTQ+ families or friends and those that do not identify with traditional identities are encouraged to participate in a GSA. Each club may be organized differently, but all GSAs work toward ensuring a supportive school environment free from harm by building a community of allies.

Gay-straight alliance clubs provide many opportunities for connection and collaboration between LGBTQ+ youth and their allies. GSAs have a positive impact on the culture of a school.

More than a Club

Gay-straight alliances generally fall into three different types of clubs: social, support, and activist. Keep in mind that an alliance can fit into one or two categories or all three. A GSA may start out as a supportive club and slowly over time, with defined leadership and goals, transition toward incorporating all three important aspects. One aspect is not better than another. However regardless of the type, it is essential that a GSA always move toward creating positive change in the community.

female appraisal different male gender inequality career lgbtq bathroom employment business diversity heterosexual unequal choice sex challenge concept discrimination family restroom toilet

UNITED WE STAND

Founded in 1998, the GSA Network was started with a goal to unite local gay-straight alliances in California. The network started with forty clubs in their region and quickly grew to over 850 GSAs. Because the network was supporting several groups in other states as well, they decided to go national. The National Association of GSA Networks supports the gay-straight alliance movement by connecting state and regional clubs with each other. The network allows alliances to interact, exchange tips, celebrate and share successes, and collaborate with others to grow the network. Registration is simple and provides clubs with different opportunities, such as monthly conference calls to discuss outreach strategies, and annual surveys that collect valuable information about the needs of GSAs around the country. Individual states can create a network for the GSAs in their region.

A social GSA answers the need for a fun and protected place for students to meet other LGBTQ+ students and allies. The meetings provide a sense of community and a space where everyone is respected. Most GSAs may start out as a social club. A social alliance is a great opportunity for teens to make friends and meet new people. Knowing that you're not alone and connecting with others who face the same struggles and strive toward the same human rights is extremely valuable. Social GSA activities would include team-building exercises or organizing a movie night or potluck.

A support GSA focuses on creating a secure space for LGBTQ+ students to disclose their emotions and struggles and to ask questions about issues they're facing at school, at home, or in their community. Activities might include check-ins that give members the opportunity to discuss or follow-up with a recent problem or having a school guidance counselor lead a discussion on issues such as mental health and body image.

An activist GSA works to improve a school's climate through direct action. Alliance actions are events organized to educate, raise awareness, and attempt to change school culture and policy. Activities may include asking a local LGBTQ+ leader from an

Movie nights with a gay-straight alliance club can be a fun social event for all to enjoy. Find films with LGBTQ+ themes, and after the movie is over start a conversation about how the film affected everyone.

advocacy group to talk about issues that may arise when preparing a campaign to raise awareness about bullying in the school or organizing an educational workshop for teachers. GSAs can incorporate all three areas of focus by alternating different monthly activities. Evaluate your school climate to determine the needs of LGBTQ+ students.

GSAs Help Keep Bullies Away

Having a safe place where LGBTQ+ students and their allies can simply express their feelings or receive support can reduce the risk of depression, substance abuse, and suicidal thoughts. A 2014 study by the University of British Columbia analyzed data from over twenty thousand Canadian students who attended schools with either anti-homophobic bullying policies or with a GSA club. The findings were somewhat surprising because gay-straight alliance clubs had a positive effect on both LGBTQ+ students and straight cisgender students. Researchers discovered that homophobic discrimination and suicidal thoughts were reduced by more than half among LGBTQ+ students in schools with a GSA compared to schools without one.

In addition, according to this study heterosexual boys were half as likely to attempt suicide as those in schools without GSAs. Schools with anti-homophobic bullying policies had a 70 percent lower rate of suicidal thoughts and attempts for gay and bisexual boys and a 27 percent lower rate of suicidal thoughts and attempts for heterosexual boys. The bottom line is that schools with gay-straight-alliances and anti-bullying policies may reduce the odds of suicidal thoughts and attempts in both LGBTQ+ students and straight cisgender students.

Every student, regardless of their gender identity or sexual orientation, deserves a safe path to graduation. GSAs and anti-bullying policies can ensure that all students are allowed to achieve their full potential.

Another study published in the November 2011 volume of *Applied Developmental Science* surveyed LGBTQ+ young adults ages twenty-one to twenty-five that had attended a school with a GSA. They were invited to discuss their experience and were asked if the GSA helped to make their school a safer and more inclusive place. The study found that LGBTQ+ students were less likely to experience depression and drop out of school. Students who participated in their school's GSA were also less likely to have problems with substance abuse and more likely to move on to college. However, the study did reveal that in schools with high levels of LGBTQ+ bullying and physical harassment, many benefits of a GSA were canceled out. The study suggested that additional action is needed in those schools, such as anti-harassment and anti-bullying policies.

MYTHS AND FACTS

Myth: GSA clubs will make students a target for bullying.

Fact: Schools with GSAs have been proved safer with decreased incidences of bullying and harassment.

Myth: Participants have to identify as LGBTQ+ to join a GSA.

Fact: Gay-straight alliance clubs are for anyone who believes in the civil rights of every human, regardless of sexual orientation or gender identity.

Myth: GSAs are recruitment or "hook-up" clubs.

Fact: Sexual orientation and gender identities are not influenced by a conversation or participation in a club activity.

CHAPTER THREE

Starting a GSA

Gay-straight alliance clubs are all across the country in cities, suburbs, and rural areas. Clubs provide support and safety for LGBTQ+ students and their straight cisgender allies. Any student interested in starting an alliance can organize one in their school. It takes just one person to initiate change in a school and make a difference. Follow a few basic steps, and rally around the excitement and passion that goes into creating a GSA.

Right off the Bat

Understanding why a GSA club is needed is essential to its future success. Students don't need a reason to start a noncurricular club, but if they are met with opposition having a clear explanation of the service a GSA can provide may help support the process. Are LGBTQ+ students enduring bullying and harassment and need a safe space to go? Or maybe LGBTQ+ students want a way to meet other students and straight cisgender allies. Take note of any specific need. Knowing the reasons why organizing a gay-straight alliance is important to the school will battle any possible resistance.

After figuring out why a GSA is needed, take time to think about a mission statement. A mission statement is one or two sentences that clearly and concisely define the group's goals and purpose. Brainstorm ideas and check out other GSA mission statements. As a group, answer questions about the GSA's goals and how to best achieve them. Discuss what the GSA stands for. Listen to all voices and ideas before coming to an agreed-upon

The initial meetings of a GSA are used to discuss the motivation for the club and to set goals for the future. Assign a member to take notes to ensure that all ideas are recorded.

statement. Allow time and patience to revise and develop the mission statement.

Place, Paperwork, and Press

Starting a GSA is just like creating any other noncurricular club. Follow any regulations or requirements outlined in the school's student handbook. If a student handbook is not available, ask an administrator who handles afterschool activities or clubs. Every school may be different. Some schools may ask for a written constitution that includes the mission statement, meeting times and locations, and the club's officers. Others schools may require permission from the appropriate staff. After figuring out what paperwork needs to be filled out and turned in, inform the administration of your plan and find a faculty adviser. An adult who has a proven record of being an ally to LGBTQ+ students is a prime choice to be the GSA adviser. This person can be a teacher or staff member such as a counselor or a librarian. More than one person can serve as an adviser.

Pick a location that is accessible to everyone, and choose a

GSAs help LGBTQ+ students and their allies identify supportive teachers and administrators. With strong support from staff, GSAs can make a real difference in a school.

time that works well, too. A location that's somewhat discreet could encourage those that might be reluctant to participate. If afterschool locations and times are too packed with other clubs or activities, try a lunchtime meeting. Once a place and time have been confirmed, it's time to get the word out!

Figure out the best way to promote the GSA, or use a combination of tried-and-true methods. Create fliers with the mission statement. Publicize the club during school announcements and direct students to a social media site to learn more. Word of mouth works well, and people will be more encouraged to participate when they talk to someone who is genuinely excited

Holding a GSA meeting in a common area and offering free food or snacks can motivate interested students to check out the club.

about the club. Offering free food is also a guaranteed way to attract participants.

Working Together

A time and place has been set, and the first meeting day has arrived! Before beginning, assign a facilitator for the meeting. The facilitator runs the meeting and guides the time according to the agenda. The initial meeting's agenda may include introductions, brainstorming ideas for future gatherings, or electing the club's leadership. Establish a group agreement that guarantees discussions are respectful and confidential. Some clubs will also agree to not use labels to ensure that everyone, however they identify, feels welcome.

The first couple of meetings are for everyone to get to know one another. This time is used to establish a safe space and develop trust. Play icebreaker games while doing introductions, such as having students introduce their preferred name and pronoun and which superpower they would want and why. Take time to think about the GSA's vision and goals. What does the club hope to accomplish in the next year? Make sure to always start and end on time and to provide free snacks. Don't forget to announce plans for the next meeting, and encourage participants to bring a friend next time.

Depending on the type of GSA, meeting activities will vary. For a social alliance, meetings might involve discussing articles or books written by LGBTQ+ activists or playing trust-building games, such as the fall back game where one person lets

LEAD WITH CONFIDENCE

Figuring out the GSA's leadership will help all club members understand their duties. Some schools will have policies regarding the club's structure or the decision may be left to club leaders. Check with the school handbook to be sure. Three different leadership structures are commonly found in a GSA: hierarchy, board, and committee.

A hierarchy-based leadership employs the standard rankings found in student body government, including a president, vice president, secretary, and treasurer. The clear and defined roles can be very effective, with each person understanding their duties and responsibilities. A GSA with a board-based structure has a selection of people who lead the club. Each member of the board has a specific responsibility, such as fund-raising or community outreach. The whole board makes decisions and everyone is accountable to each other. In committee-based leadership, specific committees are created to take care of specific needs. The events committee organizes activities and fund-raisers, while the membership committee figures out how to increase participation. GSAs can use a combination of leadership structures or these can change over time as the group determines what works best each year.

themselves fall back into the arms of another person. A support GSA meeting might figure out a support system and procedure to follow when LGBTQ+ students face discrimination or bullying. An activist meeting might identify the GSA's action plan that includes which issues they want to focus on, such as implementing stronger anti-bullying school policies or having a rally to support LGBTQ+ students of color.

Succeeding Together

Each GSA should have short-term and long-term goals. Remember, it is important to always strive toward creating a safe and inclusive environment inside and outside of school. Brainstorm and discuss which issues need action now and which will take time to accomplish. Create a short survey that asks students about problems your GSA wants to find solutions for, such as battling anti-LGBTQ+ language or teacher indifference. The information from the survey can help shape and prioritize goals.

Knowing the GSA's objectives will help guide the club toward success, but making SMART goals will really make a difference. The acronym SMART stands for specific, measurable, attainable, realistic, and timely. With each goal, the GSA should implement a strategic plan that includes assigned responsibilities, steps to take, and possible challenges that may come up. A social GSA may have a short-term goal of increasing club participation, with a long-term goal of organizing a LGBTQ+ pride parade. Reaching goals takes time, effort, and perseverance. But don't forget to celebrate successes along the way.

CHAPTER FOUR

STAND UP, SPEAK UP, AND STOP HATE

Whether debunking a common myth about GSAs or stepping in when anti-gay slurs are heard, there are several ways to be an ally to the LGBTQ+ community. An ally is a person who stands against oppression and fights for the civil rights of all people. An ally advocates for the LGBTQ+ community, fighting oppression and suppression. An ally can be a white person who speaks out against racism. Or an ally can be a straight cisgender person fighting to end transphobia. But the most critical quality of a good ally is being proactive. Sometimes an ally will offer only words, but not action. Good intentions are nice, but it's important to follow through with action. Leading others by example has a lasting and powerful effect.

Love Knows no Gender

Transgender and gender-nonconforming students often face discrimination from classmates, teachers, and sometimes even family members. Often the hate comes from fear or misunderstanding. A good ally to transgender students helps educate and increase gender identity awareness.

There are steps that a GSA can take to make sure transgender students feel welcome. Even if the club doesn't have participants that identify as transgender or gender-nonconforming, it is important to educate students to help make school a safer place. Practice using gender-neutral pronouns. Don't assume a person's preferred gender pronoun. Always ask first. Allies to transgender and gender-nonconforming students understand that there are many ways that gender is expressed. A good ally respects and accepts the beautiful diversity found in the world and encourages all people to freely express themselves.

A good ally will see all the opportunities to be more inclusive at school. The school environment can perpetuate the idea of gender as either male or female by having boys' and girls' bathrooms and an expected dress code. Allies pay attention to the

There are resources online to help allies become more proactive as they support LGBTQ+ students at their school. The allies can share what they've found with the GSA, as well as with supportive staff members.

way students talk and act, such as using gender specific language or telling a peer to act more masculine or feminine. A good ally will pick up on these occurrences and work to educate others about these gender assumptions. School can be a difficult place when you're surrounded by the gender binary. Even going to the bathroom or locker room can be a source of stress. A teen ally

STRAIGHT BUT NOT NARROW

Straight allies can be a powerful and supportive voice in LGBTQ+ advocacy. It is essential that GSAs use the support of their straight cisgender allies. These allies can stop homophobic and transphobic remarks, jokes, and bullying. Straight allies can help raise awareness. A supportive ally makes a personal commitment to stay up-to-date on current events and read articles written by LGBTQ+ authors.

Straight But Not Narrow (SBNN) is a leading ally organization that provides straight cisgender students with the resources and leadership to be powerful allies to their LGBTQ+ peers. SBNN has partnered with The Trevor Project (a crisis intervention and suicide prevention service to LGBTQ+ youth) and human-I-T (a technology donation center) in a campaign called Power On. They have asked people to donate working and nonworking

(Continued on the next page)

(Continued from the previous page)

laptops and cell phones. They refurbish the digital technology and send it off to LGBTQ+ youth who live in rural areas and do not have access to online resources. Together they've distributed a total of ten thousand cell phones and laptops.

Actor Josh Hutcherson (*second from left*) helps celebrate the money raised at the third annual Celebrity Basketball Game benefitting Straight But Not Narrow, an organization of allies supporting the LGBTQ+ community.

should offer support in environments that can be challenging or where harassment is likely. Buddy-up and go with LGBTQ+ students to places that feel unsafe or cause stress. Besides offering personal support, an ally is aware of transgender issues and strives to make lasting changes in the school. A good way to help is to campaign to create unisex bathrooms in school or develop gender sensitivity training for teachers and students.

Embrace Diversity, End Discrimination

Sometimes when people think of the word "gay" they automatically think of a white male. This common perception can be damaging. Be aware of the misrepresentation to ensure that your GSA is inclusive of all racial minorities in the LGBTQ+ community.

A 2013 report from the National Coalition of Anti-Violence Programs reported that 72 percent of victims of anti-LGBTQ+ homicide were transgender women, and 67 percent of those victims were transgender women of color. LGBTQ+ students of color are bullied based on race, gender identity, and sexual orientation.

There are many ways to be a good ally to racial minorities in the LGBTQ+ community of students in school. Speak up when hearing racist language or jokes. A good ally will recognize and reflect on privilege—a special advantage or right that's available to a select group. Pay attention to advantages and disadvantages that students face based on race, sexual orientation, or gender identity. Organize an anti-slur campaign that raises awareness of slights and offensive actions and unites the school to commit to change. Celebrate and honor LGBTQ+ leaders of color in history. Recognize cultural heritage months, such as Black History Month and National American Indian Heritage Month.

Open-Door Policy

A successful and inclusive GSA opens its doors to people of different backgrounds and addresses issues such as sexism, classism, ageism, and environmental injustice. Remember, being an ally is

On February 8, 2016, the White House celebrated Black History Month with a student dance performance honoring the contributions that African American women have made to the dance community.

about believing in and advocating for the equal rights of all people.

Just as there is homophobic language, ableist words are discriminative words used toward people with disabilities. Using words like lame, retarded, crazy, or psycho are offensive and hurtful. Take care to explain why this language is harmful. Make sure your GSA location is also accessible to those in wheelchairs. Confirm that any planned activities and events are accessible to everyone. GSAs can also incorporate LGBTQ+ people with disabilities in all educational materials.

Follow the lead of the very first GSA by making sure to include students with LGBTQ+ parents or family members. Straight cisgender students with family members or friends in the LGBTQ+ community or students who are perceived as gay are also victims of homophobic and transphobic harassment and bullying. It is important for GSAs to welcome students with LGBTQ+ family members and recognize them as part of the LGBTQ+ community. Make everyone feel welcome and do not question why they joined. And don't forget to be inclusive of adult allies in the school community. Youth-adult partnerships create a safer and more inclusive school environment. Built on mutual trust, adult allies can help battle ageism, which is when someone is discriminated against based on age. Adult allies can be an authoritative voice when battling opposition from school officials.

10 GREAT QUESTIONS TO ASK A SUCCESSFUL GSA PRESIDENT

1. How are you an effective leader?

2. How do you stay connected and informed on LGBTQ+ issues?

3. How do you increase participation in your school's GSA?

4. How do you increase diversity in a GSA?

5. How do you have difficult conversations, such as calling out a friend who uses anti-LGBTQ+ language?

6. What is the best way to handle conflict resolution in a GSA, such as when members disagree?

7. How does a GSA handle harassment and bullying?

8. How do you keep the momentum of action during the summer months?

9. What are ways to evaluate the GSA and its work?

10. What are the most useful resources for a GSA and its leadership?

CHAPTER FIVE

RISING ABOVE

GSAs can reduce discrimination and bullying in schools and help cultivate leadership in the LGBTQ+ community. However GSAs will come across challenges. Clubs may encounter obstacles, such as resistance or lack of attendance. Understanding the challenges and how to tackle each problem is part of organizing any school club. Don't let it discourage your school from starting a GSA. There are several ways to troubleshoot these problems and find success.

Keep the Ball Rolling

Gay-straight alliances foster strong relationships between LGBTQ+ students and their allies. However, sometimes a GSA will face apathy in their community or school. Apathy is when someone has no interest or concern and is indifferent to the issues LGBTQ+ students face every day. Administrators may suggest that action is not needed or that the school climate is fine. Apathy happens when a school tolerates its LGBTQ+ students but doesn't recognize the needs of the community or actively work toward promoting acceptance and inclusiveness.

The best way to deal with a lack of support from students and staff is by involving the entire school in the GSA. Ask adult allies to help publicize the GSA and its numerous opportunities to get involved. Collaborate with other clubs by organizing events together. This will give students who may

When starting a GSA, you might face resistance from students and staff members. Brainstorm ways to deal with conflicts and setbacks so you're not caught off guard should difficulties arise.

not have heard about the GSA, or who may have been hesitant to join, a chance to learn more about the alliance. Increasing visibility will help to set aside any negative assumptions. Form coalitions with clubs that align with the GSA's mission and goals, such as social justice or civil rights clubs. A coalition is a group of organizations that unite around mutual goals. Choose clubs that share a common issue and will respect the GSA's interests.

Another way to beat apathy is to start an editorial page for the school newspaper. Articles can be about why a GSA is needed or can identify and discuss LGBTQ+ issues. This route is a great way to get the word out and reach a broader audience.

Hate-Free Zone

LGBTQ+ students can experience resistance and bullying from both peers and teachers. Identifying a support system and specific procedures will help when encountering discrimination. First, secure a team of teacher and staff allies—adults that are aware of the hostility LGBTQ+ students face and are willing to do something about it. Having teachers in your corner will help if action is needed, especially if opposition is coming from other school officials. Work with teacher allies to schedule training and educational seminars that address LGBTQ+ issues. Ask if the adult ally would be willing to talk with teachers who are hostile. Sometimes teachers are more willing to listen to another adult rather than a student.

If the GSA is facing resistance, ask allies from other social justice clubs for help. It's important to show that a GSA is about the civil rights of all people, not just LGBTQ+ students. Discrimination can be a result of lack of education, so start a campaign with other social justice clubs to inform the school community of LGBTQ+ issues. If the GSA meeting place or publicity material is vandalized, laminate posters to help them last longer and hang them in a protected place, such as class-rooms or on a bulletin board. Meeting in a location that's out of

Being bullied can make a teen feel very isolated. A safe space, such as a gay-straight alliance, can provide students with an opportunity to openly discuss the harassment they've been experiencing.

the way can help, too. But remember, it is within a student's right to organize and attend a GSA. If the harassment continues, report it to authorities.

Individual LGBTQ+ students often face violence and bullying. Having a support system in place gives harassed students the assurance that the GSA has got their back. First, file a formal written complaint about the incident. Present the written report to the proper school official and ask for a solution. It is important to make sure action is taken, and don't forget to follow up. If the harassment continues, inform the school official again. If the school fails to appropriately respond, take it to the next level. At this point, it is helpful to get assistance from an adult ally who can help with further actions, such as filing a complaint with the school district. It's also useful to have a list of adult allies or hotlines to call and to make complaint forms available at GSA meetings.

Sometimes hostility can happen inside a GSA. Not everybody gets along, and just because two people identify as gay or transgender doesn't mean they will be best friends. This is OK. It is not realistic to pressure everyone in the LGBTQ+ community to like each other. But despite personality differences, it is important to stand united.

LGBTQ+ Rights Are Human Rights

A GSA is like any other noncurricular club, but organizers may encounter resistance when establishing the alliance or promoting events. Facing a "No" right off the bat can be discouraging, but remember it is within a student's right to form a club. The Federal Equal Access Act states that school administration cannot deny the organization of a gay-straight alliance. The law also states that schools can't discriminate against GSAs or treat them any differently from other noncurricular clubs. Administrators can't refuse to establish a GSA based on the assumption that they are

US Education Secretary Arne Duncan speaks at the first Federal Bullying Prevention Summit in Washington, DC, on August 10, 2010. In his talk Duncan stressed that when students feel threatened they cannot learn

"controversial" or deny a GSA the right to publically announce their group. In addition, the First Amendment protects the right to speak freely and to come together in public or private groups.

Another resource to use when facing opposition is the letter written by US Secretary of Education Arne Duncan. Written in 2011, the letter clearly states that GSAs are protected under the Equal Access Act and encourages every school district to understand that student rights are protected, regardless of sexual orientation or gender identity. It's also wise to research the laws that pertain to noncurricular clubs and anti-discrimination in your state. Contact the local GSA Network or the American Civil Liberties Union (ACLU) if questions come up. The ACLU is a national nonprofit that works to defend and preserve the constitutional rights of all Americans. Remember, LGBTQ+ rights are human rights.

CARRYING THE WEIGHT OF THE WORLD

GSAs promote inclusiveness regardless of someone's ability, class, or religion. Sometimes LGBTQ+ youth and their allies feel the need to choose between their religion and participating in a GSA. Part of the role of an inclusive alliance is the responsibility to bring respect to difficult and sensitive topics, such as religion. Ensure all students, religious or not, that a GSA is a safe place to talk about the internal conflicts that may arise when navigating religion. Welcome discussion, but set ground rules that no religion bashing is allowed. Invite guest speakers from affirming religious groups to speak. A growing number of organized religious groups have officially welcomed the LGBTQ+ community and proudly stand up for their LGBTQ+ congregation.

Cover all Bases

Suppose that the gay-straight alliance is all set, but the participation is less than expected. No one is showing up or the same two or three people attend the meetings every week. There are a few ways to successfully recruit new members. Give enthusiastic and informative presentations at other clubs' meetings, and invite those clubs to come over to the GSA to talk about their organization. Social media is a great free resource that allows a GSA to connect with many students. Create a Facebook page or Instagram account. You can make an events page that lists previous and upcoming events and post pictures, quotes, and stories from participants. Also, reevaluate the time and place of the scheduled meeting. Perhaps it is competing with too many other activities. Or change from having a weekly meeting to holding them every other week or even once a month. Consider having lunchtime gatherings because everyone has to eat lunch so it's a good time to catch students.

Tempt students with food. It may sound simple, but sweet treats or savory nibbles attract people. The free food may get them in the door, and fun planned activities will keep them engaged. Watch a LGBTQ+ movie or documentary while serving popcorn. Another good idea is to switch up meetings by alternating casual social activities with educational activities. One week, the group can play icebreaker games and the next week the club can offer a workshop on transgender awareness. It's essential to show participants that the GSA is not only an educational opportunity, but also a way to meet new friends and connect with the LGBTQ+ community.

CHAPTER SIX

THE BIG PICTURE

The number of GSAs organized across the United States keeps growing. The National GSA Network has a goal of organizing a network in every state by 2020. Work still needs to be done to support and advocate for LGBTQ+ youth. But the fact that work remains means that there are many opportunities to help the movement grow as it heads into the future.

Passing The Torch

Sustaining a GSA over time takes planning and work. Students graduate and as the next generation of LGBTQ+ students arrives, it is vital to provide the guidance and support needed for transitioning leadership. It would also be sad to see a thriving GSA come to an end because former leaders left future leaders without any help.

Chances are the teachers and staff who serve as advisers will remain with the GSA, but it never hurts to verify that they are still on board and excited about the upcoming year. At the same time, keep an eye out for potential GSA leaders. Have specific students expressed an interest in leadership? Or maybe there is an ideal candidate but that person feels unsure of their own potential. Every GSA member is a possible new leader. Regardless of the structure, having a plan in place for transitioning leadership is a good idea. If current GSA officers are approaching graduation, start training and planning for the next batch of leaders. Plan to have board or officer elections before graduation to allow

A strong leader is essential to the success of a GSA. Effective leadership requires strong communication skills, a commitment to the club, and a positive attitude.

the new GSA leaders to shadow the previous leaders as they learn the ropes. Some schools hold elections in the spring so that there is plenty of time for mentorship.

One of the most important tools to leave behind is a resource binder of all the different documents used over the years. If all else fails, the new leaders will have the resources on hand to help them have a successful year. The resource binder should include: local and national manuals and hotlines, established ground rules, previous flyer designs, a copy of the school handbook, copies of legal supportive documents such as the Federal Equal Access Act, harassment and bullying complaint forms, and any other document that may be helpful. In addition, remember to do an end-of-the-year evaluation. Have each GSA officer or board member write down what worked and didn't work during their term and how they overcame challenges. This information will give future leaders a chance to see what areas need improvement and allow them to follow the actions that supported a successful GSA.

Funding For Your GSA

GSAs can host some exciting, food-filled meetings, but clubs can't offer a single cupcake if they don't have the money to buy them. There are several fun and easy ways to raise money for GSA activities and events. Knowing how to raise money is vital to the success of a sustainable club. A hierarchy-based leadership will elect a treasurer who will be in charge of financial matters, but all leaders and GSA members should participate in fund-raising.

Each school will have its own fund-raising policies. Learn the rules and follow them. Set aside a meeting to explain to members what fund-raising is, why it's essential, and how everyone can get involved. Brainstorm different ways to raise money. Funding can come from simply placing a donation jar in a classroom or from selling candy bars or holding a bake sale. GSAs can also raise money by organizing a fund-raiser.

A bake sale is not only a great way to fund future educational events, but it can also bring awareness to the activities and goals of the GSA.

Planning a fund-raising event takes a lot of time and work, but it can be well worth it. Not only can the event bring funds to the GSA, but it can also raise awareness about LGBTQ+ issues. To organize a fund-raiser, figure out the funding goal, the steps needed to reach that goal, and who is responsible for each step. To get a high level of participation, make the objective clear and concise—what is the purpose of the fund-raiser? Local businesses may be willing to donate items or services for a silent auction. Even local restaurants can sponsor events by providing free food.

GOING NATIONAL

Every summer GSA activists from across the country unite at the National Gathering. Hosted by the National Association of GSA Networks, the event provides the opportunity to exchange success stories, share resources, and work toward building the GSA movement. The event's location changes every year and there have been gatherings all over the country. The multi-day event includes workshops, guest speakers, training, and social events. Some topics discussed in workshops include racial justice, fund-raising, and youth leadership models. Attending the National Gathering would be an ideal opportunity for a GSA leader who wishes to continue their LGBTQ+ activism beyond high school.

Having a strong and succinct objective will encourage more people to donate. When approaching potential supporters, narrow your fund-raiser description to a few sentences that include the name of the event, why you're having the event, and the ways in which their donations will help, such as raising awareness about discrimination in schools. Always thank all supporters or participants for contributing to the event. After the fund-raiser, don't forget to evaluate how it went, but most important, celebrate the success!

Rally Around

There are several different opportunities throughout the year for GSAs to celebrate and honor the LGBTQ+ community. Nationally celebrated events include Black Future Legends Month, LGBTQ+ Latinx History Month, and Ally Week. Ally Week celebrates and recognizes what it means to be an LGBTQ+ ally. GSA members share stories about their supportive allies and reflect on how to nurture and grow stronger allyships. One great idea is to hold an ally workshop that educates participants on how they can become a better ally to LGBTQ+ students. Register with GLSEN's Ally Week for free resources that include tips for a successful week and workshop ideas.

September is LGBTQ+ Latinx History Month, a time when GSAs honor and celebrate the many LGBTQ+ Latinx who have made a difference in the community. One such Latinx is Sylvia Rivera. Rivera fought for LGBTQ+ rights at the 1969 Stonewall Riots, which was a protest that helped start the LGBTQ+ civil rights movement in the United States. She was also a founding member of the Gay Liberation Front and Gay Activist Alliance, two groups that were formed shortly after the riots in support of the movement. During LGBTQ+ Latinx Month organize a poster art competition that celebrates the unique contributions of that community. Invite students to design a poster with their favorite LGBTQ+ Latinx leader and exhibit the art in the library or in a hallway display case.

Every February, the country celebrates Black History Month. The GSA Network encourages GSAs to recognize Black Future

On June 27, 2016, New York City Mayor Bill de Blasio spoke at the dedication ceremony designating The Stonewall Inn as a national monument to LGBTQ+ rights.

Legends Month—a celebration that honors Black LGBTQ+ legends who set the foundation for and inspired the next generation of legends. Too often LGBTQ+ students of color are pushed out of school. When a student is pushed out of school it is different from when a student drops out of school. Because of homophobic or racist bullying, LGBTQ+ students of color are pushed out and stop going to school because it is not a safe and supportive environment. Get involved by standing up and speaking out against racial injustice and oppression. Have a meeting to discuss what issues LGBTQ+ youth of color face and figure out ways to help. Find ways to celebrate and honor current and past LGBTQ+ leaders of color, such as Pulitzer Prize winner and civil rights activist Alice Walker.

Others days to consider celebrating are Transgender Day of Remembrance and GLSEN's Day of Silence. On November 20 of every year Transgender Day of Remembrance honors the memory of those lives that were lost in acts of anti-transgender violence. Use this opportunity to raise awareness of hate crimes against transgender people. Often LGBTQ+ groups will host a vigil that includes reading a list of the names of those that died that year. GLSEN's Day of Silence is a national event when students across the country take a vow of silence in an effort to raise awareness and put an end to anti-LGBTQ+ behavior. Schools in all fifty states have participated.

Building the GSA Movement

Much work still needs to be done in the US and international LGBTQ+ community. There are many opportunities to be a part of the movement in high school and beyond. Increased visibility of LGBTQ+ youth in schools is needed to ensure inclusive classrooms. Also, recognizing that teens play a very important role in change is essential to building the GSA movement. Today's GSA leaders can be tomorrow's LGBTQ+ community activists or politicians working towards policy change. Schools are still not free from harm, and anti-bullying policies need to be implemented everywhere. Homosexuality is still illegal in some countries, and some places it's illegal to even promote LGBTQ+ advocacy.

The passion and experience gained from organizing and participating in a high school GSA can be used in all areas of life. Do you want to carry the torch into your community? Check out internships at social justice or LGBTQ+ advocacy groups or organizations. A great way to contribute is to become a leader for change in your city or town. Work with your local government to change policy. Stay in contact with your alma mater's GSA and offer to mentor future GSA leaders. But the most vital thing to remember is that every day is an opportunity to be an ally to the LGBTQ+ community.

GLOSSARY

ACTIVIST A person who takes action in support of a political or social change.

ADVOCACY To publicly speak and write in support of a cause or issue.

AGENDER A person who does not identify with any gender. Also called genderless, genderfree, or non-gendered.

ALLY A person who supports and protects the human rights of the LGBTQ+ community.

ALMA MATER A school, college, or university which a person attended and graduated from.

ASEXUAL A person who lacks sexual attraction to anyone or who has very little to no interest in sexual activities.

CISGENDER A person whose gender identity is consistent with the gender they were assigned at birth.

COALITIONS Groups of organizations that unite around mutual goals.

CONGREGATION A group of people who worship together.

DISCRIMINATION Unfair negative treatment of a person based on race, sexual orientation, gender identity, or age.

DIVERSITY Having people from different backgrounds, cultures, races, or gender identities in a group.

FUND-RAISING Collecting money or services to support a specific cause or issue.

GENDER BINARY An assumption that there are only two gender identities, male and female.

GENDER EXPRESSION A person's outward expression through behavior, clothing, speech, or style that corresponds with their identity as male or female.

GENDER IDENTITY A person's intuitive sense of gender.

HARASSMENT Abusive and offensive words or actions aggressively and repeatedly used to intimidate a person.

HETEROSEXUAL A person who is emotionally, physically, and or sexually attracted to the opposite sex, also called straight.

HOMOPHOBIA An irrational dislike of or prejudice against homosexual people.

INCLUSIVE Including everyone, regardless of race, sexual orientation, gender identity, or age.

PANGENDER A person who relates to all genders.

PANSEXUAL A person who is emotionally, romantically, physically, and/or sexually attracted to all members of gender identities or expressions.

QUEER A comprehensive term that relates to the entire LGBTQ+ community.

SEXUAL ORIENTATION A person's preference of sexual, romantic, or physical attraction toward others.

TRANSGENDER A person whose gender identity is inconsistent with the gender assigned at birth.

TRANSPHOBIC An irrational dislike of or prejudice against transgender people.

Eagle Canada Human Rights Trust
185 Carlton Street
Toronto, ON M5A 2K7
Canada
(888) 204-7777
Website: https://egale.ca
Eagle Canada Human Rights Trust is a national charity promoting LGBTQ+ human rights through research, education, and community activities.

Gay, Lesbian & Straight Education Network (GLSEN)
110 William Street, 30th Floor
New York, NY 10038
(212) 727-0135
Website: http://www.glsen.org
GLSEN is an educational organization focused on ensuring safe and supportive schools for LGBTQ+ students.

GSA Network
1611 Telegraph Avenue, Suite 1002
Oakland, CA 94112
(415) 552-4229
Website: https://gsanetwork.org
GSA Network is an organization that empowers youth leaders to advocate for safer schools.

Human Rights Campaign
1640 Rhode Island Avenue NW

Washington, DC 20036

(202) 628-4160

Website: http://www.hrc.org/

Human Rights Campaign is a national civil rights organization
working toward assuring basic equal rights for all LGBTQ+
people.

Pride Education Network

Box 93678

Nelson Park PO

Vancouver, BC V6E 4L7

Canada

604 345-6835

Website: http://pridenet.ca/

The Pride Education Network strives to make the British
Columbia school system more welcoming and equitable for
LGBTQ+ students and staff, as well as queer families.

Websites

Because of the changing nature of internet links, Rosen Publishing
has developed an online list of websites related to the subject of
this book. This site is updated regularly. Please use this link to
access the list:

http://www.rosenlinks.com/LGBTQG/gsa

Barrett, Dawson. *Teenage Rebels: Stories of Successful High School Activists, From the Little Rock 9 to the Class of Tomorrow.* Portland, OR: Microcosm Publishing, 2015

Dawson, James. *This Book Is Gay.* Naperville, IL: Sourcebooks, 2015.

Fonda, Jane. *Being a Teen: Everything Teen Girls & Boys Should Know About Relationships, Sex, Love, Health, Identity & More.* New York, NY: Random House Publishing Group, 2014.

Gitlin, Martin. *Chaz Bono* (Transgender Pioneers). New York, NY: Rosen Publishing, 2017.

Hill, Katie Rain. *Rethinking Normal: A Memoir in Transition.* New York, NY: Simon & Schuster Books for Young Readers, 2015.

Konigsberg, Bill. *Openly Straight.* New York, NY: Scholastic, 2013.

Kuklin, Susan. *Beyond Magenta: Transgender Teens Speak Out.* Somerville, MA: Candlewick Press, 2014.

Macgillivray, Ian K. *Gay-Straight Alliances: A Handbook for Students, Educators, and Parents.* New York, NY: Routledge, 2014.

Meyer, Stephanie H., John Meyer, and Heather Alexander. *Bullying Under Attack: True Stories Written by Teen Victims, Bullies & Bystanders.* Deerfield Beach, FL: Health Communications, 2013.

Miceli, Melinda. *Standing Out, Standing Together: The Social and Political Impact of Gay-Straight Alliances.* New York, NY: Routledge, 2013.

Staley, Erin. *Laverne Cox* (Transgender Pioneers). New York, NY: Rosen Publishing, 2017.

BIBLIOGRAPHY

American Civil Liberties Union. "GSA Mission Statements Examples." Retrieved October 1, 2016. https://www.aclu.org /other/gsa-mission-statement-examples.

Belge, Kathy, and Marke Bieschke. *Queer: The Ultimate LGBT Guide for Teens*. Boston, MA: Houghton Mifflin Harcourt, 2011.

Duncan, Arne. "Key Policy Letters from the Education Secretary and Deputy Secretary." Retrieved October 14, 2016. http:// www2.ed.gov/policy/elsec/guid/secletter/110607.html.

GLSEN."Ally Week: Actions for Allies." Retrieved October 13, 2016. http://www.glsen.org/allyweek/betterallies.

GLSEN. "Being a Better Ally to LGBT Youth of Color." Retrieved October 13, 2016. http://www.glsen.org/allyweek/betterallies /studentsofcolor.

GLSEN. "Jump Start Your GSA Guide." Retrieved October 12, 2016. http://www.glsen.org/jumpstart.

GSAFE. "Building your GSA." Retrieved September 28, 2018. https://www.gsafewi.org/resources/for-youth-gsas /building-your-gsa.

GSAFE. "Fundraising Ideas for Your GSA." Retrieved October 14, 2016. http://www.gsafewi.org/resources/for-youth-gsas /building-your-gsa/fundraising-ideas-for-your-gsa/.

GSA Network. "Creating Inclusive GSAs—The Basics." Retrieved October 1, 2016. https://gsanetwork.org/resources /creating-inclusive-gsas/creating-inclusive-gsas-basics.

GSA Network. "Dealing with Hostility & Opposition." Retrieved September 24, 2016. https://gsanetwork.org/resources /building-your-gsa.

GSA Network. "GSA Network 2016-2017 Year Start Packet." Retrieved October 12, 2016. https://gsanetwork.org/resources.

Jennings, Kevin. "A Note From Kevin Jennings." Retrieved September 23, 2016. http://www.americaspromise.org /note-kevin-jennings.

Lambda Legal. "Know Your Rights: Gay-Straight Alliances." Retrieved September 27, 2016. http://www.lambdalegal.org /know-your-rights/article/youth-gay-straight-alliances.

Marx, RA, and HH Kettrey. "Gay-Straight Alliances Are Associated with Lower Levels of School-Based Victimization of LGBTQ+ Youth: A Systematic Review and Meta-analysis," *Journal of Youth And Adolescence* 45 (2016).

National Coalition Of Anti-Violence Programs. "Lesbian, Gay, Bisexual, Transgender, Queer, And HIV-Affected Hate Violence 2013 Report." Retrieved Oct 1, 2016. http://www .avp.org/storage/documents/2013_ncavp_hvreport_final.pdf.

Saewyc, Elizabeth. "School Based Strategies to Reduce Suicidal Ideation, Suicide Attempts and Discrimination Among Sexual Minority and Heterosexual Adolescents in Western Canada." *International Journal of Child, Youth & Family Studies* 5 (2014).

StopBullying.gov. "Bullying and LGBT Youth." Retrieved September 24, 2016. https://www.stopbullying.gov/at-risk /groups/lgbt/index.html.

Toomey, Russell B., et al. "High School Gay–Straight Alliances (GSAs) and Young Adult Well-Being: An Examination of GSA Presence, Participation, and Perceived Effectiveness," *Applied Developmental Science* 15 (2011).

About the Author

Kristina Lyn Heitkamp is a Montana-based author, researcher, and environmental journalist. She earned a bachelor of arts in English from the University of Utah and a masters of arts in environmental journalism from the University of Montana. She is a freelance researcher for National Geographic Books and a regular contributor to the children's magazine *Muse*. Heitkamp is committed to fighting for the basic human rights of the LGBTQ+ community. When she's not participating in an LGBTQ+ pride run with her transgender brother, she can be found writing fiction stories that explore gay-straight alliances.

Photo Credits: